MW00415976

Serial

HOMICIDE

(Volume 2)

Notorious Serial Killers Series

by: RJ PARKER

"This is a work of nonfiction. No names have been changed, no characters invented, no events fabricated."

– RJ Parker Publishing

Serial

HOMICIDE

(Volume 2)

Notorious Serial Killers Series

by: RJ PARKER

ISBN-13: 978-1987902204
ISBN-10: 1987902203

Copyright and Published (12.2016)
by RJ Parker Publishing, Inc.
Published in United States of America

Copyrights

This book is licensed for your personal enjoyment only. All rights reserved. No part of this publication can be reproduced or transmitted in any form or by any means without prior written authorization from RJ Parker Publishing, Inc. The unauthorized reproduction or distribution of a copyrighted work is illegal. Criminal copyright infringement, including infringement without monetary gain, is investigated by the FBI and is punishable by fines and federal imprisonment.

Table of Contents

1. JOHN WAYNE GACY...7
2. DENNIS RADER...23
3. EDWARD THEODORE GEIN.........................39
4. AILEEN WUORNOS.......................................55
5. JANE TOPPAN...71
6. NANNIE DOSS..87
Serial Homicide (Volume 1)...............................104
About the Author..106
Contact Information..108
References..109

1. JOHN WAYNE GACY

The Killer Clown

"The dead won't bother you, it's the living you have to worry about" - John Wayne Gacy

Introduction

John Wayne Gacy was one of America's most wanted and dangerous serial murderers and rapists, who was also infamously known as the 'Killer Clown', mainly due to his frequent participation in events for raising funds, during festive parades and at children's get-togethers, as 'Pogo the Clown', a chilling image which he had formed for himself. During the mid and late seventies, over thirty-three young adults, mainly teenage boys, were murdered by Gacy, terrorising the citizens of Cook County in Illinois. His usual methods of murder included strangulation, stabbing, asphyxiation and sexual assault.

Childhood and Background

John Wayne Gacy was born in Chicago, Illinois, on March 17, 1942, to parents of Danish and Polish descent. He was the brother to two sisters, with whom he shared a healthy relationship, along with his mother as well. Since childhood, Gacy was overweight and physically inactive. He had an abusive and rather harsh relationship with his father, who was a chronic alcoholic and engaged in domestic violence with his three children as well as his wife.

Throughout his childhood, Gacy faced assault and abuse from his father. He used to be verbally as well as physically tortured by his alcoholic father, who continuously compared him with his sisters as being the less intelligent one, and was often physically to all three of them, with a razor strop. Often his mother was abused by her husband, who accused her of upbringing the children in the wrong way and not disciplining them. Through the entire course of his childhood, Gacy strived to win his father's approval, but failed, and was always disregarded by his father. Since the age of four, he was often brutally beaten up by his father whenever his father sensed disobedience. This aggressive and abusive relationship scarred the majority of Gacy's childhood and adulthood, and though he always felt hostile towards his father, during his actual interviews in later life, he was in complete denial of holding any amount of grudge against his father.

During his early adolescence, Gacy got involved in minor cases of molestation and was sexually assaulted by a member of the family, a truck driver who was a contractor and often molested him. Gacy's schooling was further affected due to a recurrent heart ailment, which further prevented him from taking part in sports, and was a constant target of abuse, bullying and mockery by fellow friends, classmates and even by children in their neighbourhood. Gacy further faced health conditions in school in the form of seizures due to a damaged appendix and missed out on several academic milestones. However, his father denied any love or affection for the boy; he believed his son was mainly performing a deceptive act for gaining sympathy and pity.

Gacy also had a brief experience in politics before moving on to work in an ambulance organisation as mortuary assistant. During those days, his residence was in an embalming room filled with deceased bodies. In one incident, Gacy recalled fondling and finding solace in caressing a deceased male body, which made him question his sexuality. His second experience of homosexuality was after his marriage when they had moved to Iowa, where a male colleague had engaged in oral sex with him after getting him drunk. By the sixties, Gacy had ascended to be the Vice President of the United States Junior Chamber, also known as the Jaycees or JCs. Later, he accepted the purchase of the restaurants run by his father-in-law and worked hard for the Jaycees. It was during this time that Gacy felt his life to be going positive and well; he even won his much-sought approval from his father, who later claimed to apologise to him for his verbally and physically abusive behaviour during childhood.

However, Gacy was also involved in several crimes during his work with the Jaycees, which involved drug abuse, prostitution, pornography and wife swapping. He engaged in several incidents of cheating on his wife and getting involved with prostitutes and molestation of teenage male employees.

Early murders

After minor incidents of molesting teenage boys and sodomy, imprisonment and clearance, and a broken marriage, Gacy married a second time and moved to a Summerdale Avenue house. Another incident followed where Gacy raped a male employee of PDM contractors in a hotel room in Florida, where they had gone to view property. He was a member of a Moose club in his locality, where he and his colleagues performed in several entertaining events as fundraisers, disguised as clowns. During 1975, Gacy got involved in a group known as Jolly Jokers, where he formulated the characters 'Patches the Clown' and 'Pogo the Clown'. He performed in several parties, fundraisers and hospitals where he applied his own make up, which was further self-taught. The make-up which Gacy applied was particularly sinister; he painted sharp corners near his mouth, unlike the more approved rounded shapes, in order to prevent children from being frightened. It was also during this time that he confessed his homosexuality to his wife, and she discovered gay pornography and Gacy accompanied by teenage boys in his garage, which was followed by divorce.

Gacy's first murders involved a 16-year-old youth named Timothy Jack McCoy, who was waiting at the bus stop in Chicago. Gacy, who was also en route to Michigan, offered to escort the boy, promising to return him home before spending the night at his house. He awoke in the morning to find McCoy holding a knife in his hand, unaware of the fact that he was preparing breakfast and slicing bacon. After a brief scuffle, Gacy killed him via multiple stabs and, upon realising his mistake, claimed to have felt 'drained'. However, he also mentioned the fact that the killing caused an orgasm and was particularly exciting for him. Another victim, who was not identified, was killed by strangulation and was kept briefly in Gacy's closet, before being buried in his backyard. He was estimated to about fourteen to sixteen years old.

His third assault was during 1975 when he worked overtime in his business of contractors, where he tried to hold a youth captive, after several other episodes of being sexually involved with young male employees. The youth, having learned wrestling, managed to escape; after escaping the handcuffs Gacy had held him in, he cuffed Gacy as well. Another murder was of seventeen-year-old John Butkovitch, who had previously threatened Gacy for his due payments. Gacy had told him to come to his home, where he applied handcuffs and strangled him to death. His parents called Gacy, who claimed that the boy had escaped after reaching a compromise regarding the payments, before finally confessing to the murder.

Gacy's Cruising years and 'The Killer Clown'

A series of other murders followed during the time which Gacy referred to as his 'cruising years'; that is, during the years of 1976 and 1978. Darrell Sampson, an 18-year-old, was kidnapped and killed after last being spotted in Chicago a month after Gacy's divorce. Another young boy, Randall Reffett, 15 years of age, was gagged with a cloth and killed by asphyxiation, while he was returning home from school. Another murder followed of a youngster named Michael Bonnin, 17 years of age. He was strangulated and buried in Gacy's crawl space. Following this was the murder of 16-year-old William Carroll, who was killed and cremated in Gacy's kitchen. Many of Gacy's victims were buried in this usual grave, which was located between his laundry room and kitchen. Several other unidentified male bodies were also uncovered in Gacy's common graveyard, one of whom had a denture and a fractured clavicle. Gacy also attempted assault and rape over another 18-year-old employee of

PDM contractors, David Cram. Prior to his attack, Cram had a year-long experience in the Army, and was able to defend himself against Gacy, following which he left the contractor's business, while working occasionally for Gacy over a period of two years.

Over the following three months of mid-1976, several other unidentified murders were committed by Gacy, one of whose bodies had a damaged tooth. Their burials, identified by Gacy's colleagues, were carried out in separate trenches, which were newly dug upon orders by Gacy. During the month of October 1976, Gacy killed another three teenagers, Michael Marino, Kenneth Parker and a 19-year-old employee named William Bundy, all of whom were killed by strangulation. All of them were buried in Gacy's infamous crawl space, which was located underneath Gacy's master bedroom.

During December of 1976, Gacy was involved in another murder, this time, a new employee of PDM contractors who had just begun working almost a month earlier. Gregory Godzik, about 17 years old, had discussed his duties at work with his family, including that he was frequently ordered to dig trenches. He was last seen by his girlfriend after he had driven her home. His car was later discovered near the

Niles. The family, on contacting Gacy, was told by him that Godzik had disappeared, and had indicated that to Gacy a few days back. Gacy claimed to have had an audio message from Godzik on an answering machine, but on being asked by the family to hear it, informed them that he had deleted it.

The next year, a friend of Godzik, John Szyc, was called by Gacy in his home, about selling his Plymouth Satellite. His body was found in Gacy's common crawl space, and a ring which had his initials engraved on it was found in Gacy's dressing table.

During the following year of 1976, Gacy was involved in several other youth murders, through kidnapping, strangulation and suffocation, where some of the victims were not identified. Their bodies were all buried in the usual crawl space of Gacy's house.

The final murders of 1978 and capture

During the early months of 1978, Gacy was involved in assaulting 26-year-old Jeffrey Rignall by luring him into his car. Upon doing so, he was rendered unconscious via chloroform and was driven to Gacy's Summerdale home, where he was continuously tortured violently and raped, again rendered unconscious and the assaults were repeated again. He was later dumped in Lincoln Park while still being alive. After struggling to make his way to his girlfriend's house and informing the police about his assault and observations, Gacy was finally arrested during July of 1978.

During his imprisonment, Gacy admitted about his usual plans of burying victims in his crawl space as well the attic. However, due to the high number of bodies, Gacy's next move was to remove the bodies to the Des Plaines River, by throwing them from the l-55 bridge. Gacy later confessed that five of his victims in 1978 were disposed of in this manner; four had been found; and another he recalled had fallen on a barge which was passing beneath the bridge during his act of throwing the corpse. Most of his victims were the usual young adults who were usually kidnapped on their way home and strangulated to death. One died due to asphyxiation of his own vomit, after his underwear was forced into his throat and he choked.

During the final months of 1978, Gacy had visited a medical store and mentioned to a young male employee, Robert Jerome Piest, that his company hired youngsters like him. Piest later informed his mother that he would talk to this potential employer and ended up not returning home. The family of Piest filed a report of disappearance to the Des Plaines police, and the pharmacy owner also claimed that it was most probably Gacy to whom Piest had gone to talk to after leaving the premises.

Gacy, however, vehemently disagreed with this, claiming that he merely asked the youth present in the store, who was Piest most probably, regarding materials for remodelling. He was asked to file his written statement that evening. The police, however, considered him as the prime suspect, in light of Gacy's previous charges of assault and sexual violation of youngsters, including the torture of 26-year-old Rignall. Upon investigating his home, several questionable items were found, some of which were a ring with engraved initials, clothes for which Gacy was too oversized, handcuffs, licenses, books and videos regarding homosexuality and gay pornography, receipts from the medical store attended by Piest, and many more, following which police continued a pressing surveillance over Gacy over the next few months.

Regarding the Rignall case, the police conducted another investigation where the report had mentioned the sexual assault and rape suffered by Rignall. Other reports included tracing the ring of high schooler Szyc, and his mother confirming the missing report, and as well a friend of Godzik, Michael Rossi, calling about the disappearance and murder of Godzik.

On the other hand, Gacy, as a defence, began to appear favourable in front of the investigators, frequently inviting them for dinners and parties and constantly claiming that he had no connection in the disappearance of Piest. He even claimed that the police and detectives were pressing too harsh charges upon him, merely due to his political party involvement and drug use. The following December, a thorough investigation was conducted on Gacy's car, where human hair strands were found and sent for further investigations. Another search followed using police dogs. One dog, lay down on the rear seat for passengers, to which police claimed that it was a reaction to death, and it was probably where the body of Piest was kept.

The continuous attention left Gacy tired and worried and he acquired heavy alcoholism. In response to the charges against him, Gacy filed a lawsuit in order the remove the charges against him. However, at the end of December, when he again met his lawyer regarding the civil suit, Gacy, upon drinking and viewing the news about Piest's disappearance, began confessing to his crime. After falling asleep and awakening again, he confessed to almost thirty of his murders. The police, in the meanwhile, had prepared a second search warrant for Gacy's house, and upon hearing that he had confessed to his lawyers and other fellow contractor colleagues, and that he might commit suicide, they decided to arrest him.

The search warrant was further confirmed and authorised by Judge Marvin Peters upon the police coming to know about the civil suit filed by Gacy. Investigators, the police and technicians now entered Gacy's home and began searching the household thoroughly. Upon investigating the infamous crawl space, decomposed flesh and bones were immediately uncovered, and Gacy was charged with murder.

The police then sat with Gacy to hear a detailed confession, and Gacy informed them about every murder, the victims and details, followed by how he murdered and buried them, and the ongoing search for the victims' bodies followed. Following the recovery of bodies, Gacy was shortly charged for over thirty-three murders.

Trial and Sentencing

Gacy was brought to court for trial, accused of over thirty-three murders. The trial was held in February, 1980, and was presided over by judges from Illinois. Before that, Gacy had undergone several psychiatric evaluations in Menard Correctional Centre, in order for doctors to find out whether he was mentally fit to come to court. Gacy tried to make the doctors believe that he was a patient of multiple personality disorders. Gacy's lawyers, on the other hand, pleaded not guilty by reason of insanity and even produced medical reports claiming the same.

Other medical reports claimed that he was suffering from paranoid schizophrenia, along with symptoms of multiple personality disorder. The prosecution, however, claimed that Gacy suffered from no mental illness as such and was completely aware of what he was doing and the crimes that he had committed. This was further backed by testimonies by a number of witness, including his employees who were ordered to dig trenches for expanding Gacy's crawl space, in the areas being marked by Gacy; other testimonies regarding how Gacy attempted to escape his charges via filing the civil suit, witnesses like Rossi and Rignall, who showed detailed diagrams of this crawl space, and the torture and rape that ensued. Certain doctors also backed the contentions of the prosecution, by producing reports which denied Gacy's claims of suffering from any form of mental disorders.

After a long deliberation stretching for over two hours, the court found Gacy guilty for thirty-three murders, including assault, molestation, rape and sexual violation of children. While the prosecution pleaded for a death sentence, the defence asked for an imprisonment for life.

Gacy was finally kept at Menard Correctional Centre where he resided for the next fourteen years. During this time, he engaged in painting, mainly of 'Pogo the Clown', which were shown at auction and exhibitions.

Gacy was executed in 1994, using lethal injection. Upon his execution, his brain was removed and sent for examination, which showed no signs of abnormalities. Some of Gacy's paintings were also sold and displayed in exhibitions. Gacy had claimed that he painted for the purpose of imparting happiness in people's lives. Some of these paintings, however, were burned during a communal meeting, which was attended by the families and friends of victims murdered by Gacy and other civilians who supported his death sentence and execution.

According to certain reports before Gacy's execution, Gacy was said to have felt no sense of guilt for his crimes and actions and was claimed to be a psychopath. It is said that in his final statement, Gacy had stated that his death sentence would not relieve the death or loss of those who had been murdered, or their families, and the state was forcibly killing him. Several civilians had come over to observe the execution, most of whom bore slogans and shirts in favour of the death sentence. There were also others present who were not in favour of the execution and merely performed a candlelight march.

2. DENNIS RADER
The BTK Killer

"When this monster entered my brain, I will never know, but it is here to stay. How does one cure himself? I can't stop it, the monster goes on, and hurts me as well as society. Maybe you can stop him. I can't." - Dennis Rader

Dennis Lynn Rader was a serial killer

from the United States of America, who was born on March 9, 1945. He actively committed ten murders during the time period spanning the seventies and early nineties, in Sedgwick County, in the state of Kansas. Rader was notoriously known as the BTK killer or BTK strangler, due to his common method of killing; that is, 'Bind, Torture and Kill'. What made his killing spree even more sinister and chilling is that during the crimes he committed, he sent every detail of the murders to neighborhood news organizations and even the police department. After his last murder, he followed a brief hiatus till the wee months of 2000s, where he again resumed sending letters. This escalated into his arrest shortly and life sentencing. He is presently residing in El Dorado Correctional Facility in Kansas, charged with ten murders and the resultant ten life sentences.

Background and Early Life

Rader was born in Pittsburgh, Kansas, and further lived his early life in Wichita. Out of the four children of William Elvin Rader and Dorothy Mae Rader, Dennis was the eldest. Based on his confessions and other childhood incidences, Radar was sadistic towards animals and gained pleasure in torturing them. He was also sexually aroused by female underwear and

24

wore the same after stealing it from his murder victims.

He joined the United States Air Force in 1966 and spent the next four years there. After that he moved to Park City and, along with his mother, worked at the Leekers IGA Supermarket. His mother worked there as a bookkeeper, while Rader joined the meat section. On 22nd March, 1971, he married Paula Dietz, with whom he had two children.

Rader completed his education in El Dorado, Butler County Community College, from where he graduated in 1973 with an Associate degree in electronics. He further continued his education in Wichita State University, from where he graduated with a Bachelor's degree in justice administration in the year of 1979.

He joined an outdoor supply company, known as the Coleman Company, where he worked as an assembler. After that he moved to Wichita in 1974 and worked in a home security organization, ADT Security Services, until 1988. His work there included installation of security alarm systems. Ironically, a number of customers sought for the company's services in the hopes of staying safe from the BTK Killer, where in actuality, it was merely an invitation for him to kill. He also worked as a supervisor for census filing operations in Wichita during 1989. Later, he worked as a compliance officer and a dog catcher in the area of Park City, in which some of the area residents regarded him as being overly stringent and over enthusiastic. One individual recalled that her dog was euthanized for no justified reason. In March 2005, after he had been arrested for five murders, the Park City council dismissed Rader from work, for lack of work and not calling in.

Rader was also a part of the Christ Lutheran Church and also won an election to be president of the church council. He was a leader of Cub Scouts. After Rader's arrest in July 2005, the District Judge of Sedgwick County took into consideration that Rader's wife, Paula, was adversely affected both mentally and physically during her years of marriage with him, and she was granted an immediate divorce, instead of facing the waiting period of sixty days.

Murders

Rader committed all of his ten murders in the state of Kansas. In all cases, not only did he murder his victims, but he also stole their valuables. All of his victims were women aged in their late twenties or mid-thirties. Most of them were killed due to strangulation and asphyxiation, while one victim was stabbed multiple times in her back and torso. The items Rader usually used for murdering included ropes, plastic bags, stockings, belts and, in some cases, even his bare hands. Rader's fetish with female underwear also made him use items like pantyhose and nylon stockings for strangling his victims. Most of his murders were carried out in Wichita and Park City.

Rader stalked women and planned to kill them. One of them included 69-year-old Anna Williams. Rader waited in her home for several hours but left before Williams returned home quite late. Another two victims stalked by Rader shifted their place of residence and filed a restraining order against him. During his interrogation, Rader confessed that he was planning to stalk and murder again after returning from his hiatus.

Most of the bodies of the victims were recovered on the day of the murder in the same location where the murder was committed. One victim, whose murder was carried out in Park City, was discovered after eight days in Wichita, between North Greenwich Road and North Webb Road. Another murder victim who was killed in Wichita was found almost after two weeks in Sedgwick County near North Meridian Street. Almost all victims were women, except for nine-year-old Joseph Otero, the youngest member of the Otero Family.

Case study and details

The primary act which earned Rader his notoriety was his sending of letters and murder details to the police and other local news report agencies. This was carried out at large during his prime murdering years from 1974 to 1979. His very first letter, found in October of 1974, was stuffed in a book of engineering in the Wichita Public Library. It described in gory detail the murder of the Otero family, committed in the month of January 1974. Another letter followed in 1978, which was sent to a television station in Wichita, wherein Rader claimed himself as the murderer of the Otero family as well as other three victims, Kathryn Bright, Nancy Fox, and Shirley Vian. In the letters, he gave numerous names as his identity, and finally stuck to what became widely known as 'BTK', an abbreviation of 'Bind, Torture and Kill'.

In another letter, Rader asked for media coverage of his killings, and that was when it was confirmed that a serial murderer was on the loose in Wichita. In the same letter, to further add to the notoriety and fear, he added a poem on the killing of Nancy Fox, which was a twisted version of a popular American country track, 'Oh Death'.

After the murder of another family in Wichita during 1988, another letter was sent. The sender identified himself as the BTK killer and felt he had done work worth the applause. It was not until 2005 that it was proven that the letter was indeed written and sent by Rader.

During 2004, the investigation to search for the BTK killer was performed in full force. Rader further contacted the local media organizations in 2005 for a total of eleven times, which ultimately led down the road to his arrest. Following the month of March 2004, a local newspaper, the Wichita Eagle, received a letter containing the details of the murder of Vicki Wegerle, which was committed in 1986, and also included pictures of the murder scene and a copy of her driver's license, all of which had been stolen after the deed was done. The writer used the name as 'Bill Thomas Killman'. During previous investigations, however, it was not proven that Wegerle was murdered by the BTK strangler. Following the letter, a number of DNA analysis reports were carried out on a number of men, but none provided the evidence needed, and, hence, the reports were destroyed later upon orders of the court.

Another letter was sent in 2004 to a television station in Wichita, KAKE, which was divided into several subparts and titled as the 'BTK Story'. A package was attached to a stop sign at First and Kansas which contained disturbing descriptions of the murder of the Otero family, with the heading 'Sexual Thrill is my Bill'. The package also contained a proposal for publishing a book about the BTK story, which clearly mocked previous investigations and television broadcasting of the same during the late eighties. The title of the first chapter was hinted at sinisterly as 'A Serial Killer is Born'. Another package followed in the month of July in a public library, which further had the sender claiming himself as the BTK killer and also contained graphic information of a murder committed during that year in Kansas, of Jake Allen, 19 years old. However, this information was regarded as false as it was proven that the death was caused by suicide.

Capture and Arrest

Another package was uncovered in a UPS box in Wichita, which contained terrifying images of child bondage and torture and a death warning to prime investigator, Lt. Ken

Landwehr. The packages also contained details of Rader's life which were later released to the public.

During the latter part of 2004, the police received another package which contained the driver's license of Nancy Fox, as well as a chilling doll with its hands and feet bound and the head covered with a plastic bag. This was found in a park in Wichita. In the following year of 2005, Rader left a cereal box in a pick-up truck in Wichita which was, however, removed by the driver shortly after. The box was searched for and found again after Rader left a message asking for its whereabouts. Videos for surveillance in that parking area later showed an individual leaving in a car after depositing the box. During the month of February, more chillingly detailed postcards were sent to the television station, and another box was found which contained another horrific looking doll, depicting the murder of Josephine Otero, 11 years old.

In one of Rader's letters which he had sent to the police, he asked if his information could be traceable if encoded in a floppy disk. The police answered affirmatively of its safe use in an advertisement printed in the newspaper, the Wichita Eagle. In February

2005, Rader sent a floppy disk to KSAS TV, affiliated to Fox TV, and the package further contained a medallion, a golden necklace, and a photocopied book cover of a serial killer novel released in 1989. However, unknown to Rader, a deleted Microsoft Word Document was found embedded in it, titled 'Christ Lutheran Church', which contained the information, "last modified by 'Dennis'." Further investigation revealed that Dennis Rader was the president of this church. Previous surveillance footage had revealed that the killer owned a Black Cherokee. Hence, when police drove to Rader's home, they found a Cherokee parked outside.

Even though the police were absolutely convinced that Rader was the prime suspect and killer, they still needed further evidence to arrest him. The police first proceeded by getting a warrant to analyze the Pap smear which Rader's daughter had taken during her student years at the Kansas State University medical clinic. Upon medical examination by the Kansas Bureau of Investigation in their Topeka lab, a match was found based on the DNA test report which was obtained from medical examination of the fingernails of murder victim, Vicki Wegerle. This information clearly proved that the murderer was associated with the family of Rader's daughter and was sufficient for the police to issue an arrest warrant.

While driving home in Park City, the police stopped Rader. After he was arrested, the police, law enforcement officials, the bomb units, the FBI, ATF. KBI agents and SWAT units undertook a search of Rader's home. After searching his home and car, several items were uncovered, such as black pantyhose, a cylindrical container and computer parts. Even his work office at City Hall and the public library were searched thoroughly. It was finally released at a press conference the following day that the Wichita police confirmed that the BTK strangler had been finally arrested.

Trial and sentencing

Rader was charged with ten murders on February 25, 2005. Various news report organizations claimed to have cited from anonymous sources that the BTK killer had confessed to his crimes. Upon being questioned, the district attorney of Sedgwick County denied the information, but he also didn't state whether Rader had truly confessed to the killings or if any more investigations and examinations were being carried out for other murders which had not yet been solved. During March, news agencies again claimed to have obtained information from various other sources that Rader had indeed confessed to the ten murders charged against him, but not the additional unsolved murders.

He appeared in court on March 1, 2005, by way of a video conference. The district judge appointed a public defender for him during the next meeting on March 15 and also stated a bail of ten million dollars. During May, the district judge entered a not guilty plea on behalf of Rader, as he had not spoken during this arraignment. However, on the initial day of the trial held in June, Rader pled guilty for all the ten charges filed against him and explained all of them in perfect detail, without any sense of emotion, guilt or remorse.

On August 18, 2005, Rader faced his sentencing. It included statements by the families of the murder victims and a speech of apology from Rader himself. The apology speech lasted for over an uncomfortable thirty minutes, which the district attorney of Sedgwick County described as that resembling an acceptance speech for the Academy Awards. Radar was sentenced to a total of ten life imprisonment sentences, a sentence for each murder committed. During the time the murders were committed, Kansas had no death penalty by law, and, hence, the highest penalty which could be rendered was a life sentence. Rader could be granted parole in the year 2180, after a total of 175 years of imprisonment.

During August, Rader was moved from Sedgwick County Jail to El Dorado Correctional Facility in Kansas. It was here where he began serving his life sentences. It was said by witnesses that, during the journey from Wichita to El Dorado, Kansas, Rader talked rather normally. However, he broke down when the statements by the family members of the murder victims began to be played in the radio. At present, Rader is residing in El Dorado Correctional Facility in Kansas. He is kept in solitary confinement, for his own protection, under the Special Management unit. He is imprisoned for over twenty-three hours per day, apart from the hour-long yard exercise routine and usage of the shower thrice every week. During 2006, despite the disapproval of the families of the victims, Rader achieved incentive level two due to good behavior. From then on, he has been permitted to access the television, read magazines and papers, and listen to the radio. However, it is likely that Rader will have to maintain this designation for the remainder of his life of imprisonment.

Other investigations

After his arrest, police turned to further investigations of other unsolved murders and crimes. With the help of the state police and FBI, the Wichita police investigated other murder cases which had been committed in other cities as well as those which had taken place after the year 1994, when the death penalty was brought back in force in Kansas. Various cases were looked into which had details similar to Rader's style of killing. These included investigation of murders in various cities in Colorado, Texas, Nebraska, Missouri and Oklahoma. Even the Air Patrol looked into other murder cases which had occurred during Rader's stint in the military.

After long driven investigations, it was finally concluded that Rader wasn't involved in any further murder, and neither had he confessed to any apart from the existing ten. It is now believed that Rader had actively taken part only in those ten murders. However, police still suspected that, apart from performing those ten murders, Rader most probably stalked other victims and planned to murder them as well. Rader himself had admitted that there were several potential victims who were lucky and escaped his attack. This included one individual from whose neighboring area Rader had to leave after considerable stalking, since there were a number of construction and road crew individuals in that area.

Following this, the public defenders for Rader, who had been previously appointed by the court, further hired Robert Mendoza, a psychologist based in Massachusetts, in the hopes that a plea for insanity can be devised. The interview had taken place after Rader had pled guilty in July. It was reported later by NBC that Rader was aware that the interview was to be broadcast on television. However, such information was deemed as false by the department of the Sheriff of Sedgwick County. Rader had even talked about the interview when he had announced his statement of sentencing and apology.

In another turn of events, on October 25, 2005, the Attorney General of Kansas filed a petition against the members of the Cambridge Forensic Consultants, Tali Waters and Robert Mendoza, with claims that their financial benefits were involved by obtaining essential information via involvement in the case for defense of Rader and a breach of the agreement. The situation was finally settled and called off during May 2007 with Mendoza not admitting to any wrong actions and closing the issue with thirty thousand dollars.

Popular culture

The case of Dennis Lynn Rader, as the BTK killer and strangler, has been documented and based in the form of several stories in several novels and films, like the 'Red Dragon' and 'A Good Marriage'. Several documentary films have also documented the BTK murders, as well as certain television programs. Several music bands based on metal and rock have also based their album and song content on the BTK murders, with titles such as Suffocation, Suicide Commando, Church of Misery and Exodus. Some of it was played during a promotional clip by the History Channel for their series titled 'The Dark Ages'.

3. EDWARD THEODORE GEIN
Cult Killer and Body Snatcher
"She isn't missing, she's at the farm right now."
- Ed Gein

Edward Theodore Gein was a murderer in the United States and was infamously known for his acts of body snatching and sinister transgressive cult- based mutilation of his stolen corpses. His crimes took place mostly in

Plainfield, Wisconsin, which was his hometown. What made Gein even more infamous was that he stole corpses from neighboring graveyards and made household items from them after tanning the skins. One of more gruesome acts included extracting the skin and bones from certain dead bodies and using them as relics and rewards for himself. He later confessed to committing two murders, in 1954 and 1957. Before appearing for trial, Gein resided in a mental health hospital where it was claimed that he was not fit to stand trial. During 1968, he was found guilty but was still ordered to be kept in a mental health hospital due to legal pleas of insanity. He died due to respiratory and liver damage caused by cancer at Mendota Mental Health Institute. His grave lies in Plainfield Cemetery, which is unmarked at present.

Background and Early life

Edward Theodore Gein was the second of two children born to Augusta Wilhelmine and George Phillip Gein. Familial strains were caused due to Gein's father being an alcoholic and unsuccessful in maintaining a stable place of work. His father worked in various jobs, as a tanner, insurance agent, and even at carpentry. He maintained a neighborhood shop selling groceries, which was sold later. Finally, the Geins moved their place of residence permanently to Wisconsin, in the small town of Plainfield.

Gein's mother was fairly strong in her Lutheran beliefs, and living in such an isolated place helped her exert her influences more on her children. She did not allow her sons to interact with any outsiders. The only time Ed had permission to go out was for attending school. Apart from that, he and his brother, spent most of their time at home doing the housework. Their mother, Augusta, took time in teaching them her beliefs, mainly regarding how harmful and evil alcoholism was, that women were generally servants of the devil and were prostitutes, and how inevitably immoral the world was. Every afternoon, she would read out to them from the Old Testament of the Bible regarding divinity, death and killing.

In school, Ed was reported to be an introvert with queer habits. Often fellow students and teachers recalled him having sudden bursts of random laughter as if reveling in the humor of his own jokes. Further, his mother prevented him from interacting or being friends with anyone. Despite the odds, Ed performed satisfactorily well in school and was especially impressive during reading.

Gein's father, George Phillip, passed away due to alcoholism-induced heart failure at the age of 66. Following this, the two brothers toiled away doing odd jobs in order to run the household and take care of their mother. The neighborhood usually found Ed and his elder brother, Henry, to be hard-working and honest. Both brothers worked as handymen in the neighborhood, while Ed, in addition, was often employed as a babysitter. Ed behaved well in the company of children as he found more comfort with them as compared to adults. At this time, Henry got into a relationship with a woman who was divorced and had two children. He was, however, wary of the love and duty Ed bore for his mother and often spoke negatively about her in front of him, which deeply shocked and hurt Ed.

During March 1944, the two brothers were incinerating unwanted vegetation in the farmland and, in the process, the fire spread. The fire brigade was called for and the fire was extinguished. However, Henry was nowhere to be found. After a search was conducted, his body was recovered with him lying face down. Reports claimed that he probably expired due to heart failure, as no burn or injury marks were found on his body. Later, in a biography about Gein, titled 'Deviant', by Harold Schechter, it was written that there were bruises on his head. While some believed that he was killed by Ed, the police and medical authorities denied such theories and believed the death may have been caused due to asphyxiation. While questioning Gein about the death of Bernice Worden, the state crime authority also asked him about the death of his elder brother, Henry, and suspected that he probably had a hand in his brother's death.

The only ones left in the family were Augusta and Ed. His mother suffered from a stroke later which left her paralyzed, and Ed had to devote all his time to her. In one incident, as reported by Gein, he and his mother had gone out to buy straw from a person named Smith. There they saw Smith beating a dog violently until it died, although a woman had tried to intervene. This scene marked a deep impact on Ed's mother, not because of the suffering animal but, in her words, the unwanted presence of the woman, whom she referred to as a harlot for being there despite not being married. She passed away after another stroke shortly after. This left Ed depressed, hurt and all alone, as his mother was the only companion and friend whom he had after the death of his father and brother, and she had meant the world to him.

Gein continued to work on the farm and also performed his usual odd jobs. He maintained his mother's room and the living room in excellent condition, while the rest of the house deteriorated. Gein himself resided next to the kitchen in a small room. It was at this stage of his life when he began to develop an interest in reading stories about Nazi killings and cannibals, and also cult magazines.

He spent his days working as a handyman and, since 1951, had been receiving a subsidy for farming from the federal government. He even got employed for crop threshing in farmlands of that area, and also often got involved in working with the road crew of the local municipality. In his later years, notably between 1946 and 1956, he sold some farmland comprising about eighty acres which was the property of his elder brother.

Murders

Gein's earliest murders went back to the year 1957, which began with the disappearance of a store owner selling hardware, Bernice Worden, on November 16. On the previous day, Worden's son reported to the police that Gein had been in the store during the evening. Gein had promised to come back to the store the next morning for some antifreeze. Hence, this made the police note Gein as the primary suspect. The last transaction of the shop, as written by Worden, was the selling of antifreeze. The police next investigated Gein's residence and property and discovered the corpse. Worden's body was found in a shed, decapitated, hanging with a crossbar in her feet and ropes tied to her hands. Her trunk was reportedly carved out 'like a deer'. Upon examination, it was found that the chilling mutilations were committed after she was killed with a shot from a .22-calibre rifle.

The police further searched Gein's house and made horrifying discoveries. These included some fingernails derived from fingers of a female, lips used as a drawstring for windowshades, a lampshade which had been made from a human face, four noses, two vulvas which upon examination were assumed to be from girls aged 15 years old, a belt which was made from human nipples, Worden's heart which was kept in a plastic bag near Gein's stove, a further nine vulvas stashed in a box, Worden's missing head in a sack, masks made from female faces, a skull in a box identified to be that of Mary Hogan, Mary Hogan's face in a bag, a corset carved out from the skin of the torso of a female body, a pair of leggings made from human skin, skulls near his bed and more female skulls with the top part removed, a basket made of human skin, and a number of human bones and body parts.

All of these remains were photographed and kept at the state crime laboratory and finally destroyed. Upon being questioned regarding the findings, Gein reported that these were acquired during the years 1947 to 1952. During this time, Gein claimed that he would be in a trancelike state and, during this state, he had visited three neighboring graveyards about forty times during the night. According to him, during thirty of these visits, he would recover from his trance state in the graveyard itself and leave the place without any action of body snatching or damaging of property. During the other moments where he maintained this 'daze-like state', he would dig up the graves of women whom he thought bore a resemblance to his mother, take the corpses home, tan their skins and create his sinister artifacts.

Gein confessed that he had tampered with about nine such graves, compelling authorities to examine the locations. They were doubtful as to whether Gein was capable on his own to dig up a grave, so they searched two graves and found that they were empty and had crowbars placed in them. The state crime laboratory exhumed three graves which were pointed out by Gein. The coffins were kept in wooden boxes where the top boards were crossways. The upper portion of the wooden box was not very deep, beneath only a two-foot layer of sandy soil, indicating that Gein tampered with fresh graves soon after the funerals were completed but the graves were not. They were discovered in the condition as described by Gein. He had failed to open one casket due to the loss of his crow bar, another one was empty, while the third one had an almost fully decomposed body, except for a few parts and rings which Gein had stolen.

Case study

After the death of his mother, Gein coped with the loss by the desire to become like her, or come into her skin, hence his habits of tanning the female skins and forming a suit. His habit of wearing such skin suits to resemble his mother was named as a transvestite cult ritual. Gein, however, claimed that he did not ever have sexual intercourse with the bodies because of their unappealing odour. During another questioning by the state crime laboratory, Gein confessed that he had shot dead Mary Hogan. Hogan was the owner of a tavern; she had mysteriously disappeared during 1954, and her head was found in Gein's house. However, during further questioning, he denied having any remembrance about her murder or death.

Gein was sometimes visited by teenaged youngster, a close associate of their family, and attended movies and ball games with him. The skulls which were found in Gein's house, he told the boy, were artifacts from the Philippines which were gifted to him by a cousin who had served there during the Second World War. Upon medical examination, they were found to be shrunken human skins to be worn as masks by Gein.

The police also suspected Gein for committing several other unidentified crimes in the area of Wisconsin, notably the disappearance of a La Crosse babysitter, Evelyn Hartley, during 1953. During the questioning of Gein, he was assaulted by the Sheriff of Waushara County, Art Schley, who shoved Gein's head and face into a brick wall. Due to this incident, Gein's first confession was ruled out due to his injuries. Ironically, Schley passed away due to heart failure in the year 1968, aged 43 years old. Schley's friends and associates claimed that he was shocked and horrified by the sinister actions of Gein. This trauma, along with the fear that he may have to appear in court for hurting Gein, all led to his heart failure and resultant death. One of his friends claimed that Schley became indirectly a victim of Gein, almost as if he had mutilated him, as he did to his victims.

Trial and Sentencing

Gein stood trial on November 21, 1957, where he was charged with one first-degree murder by the court in Waushara County. Gein did not plead guilty, citing insanity as a reason. He was later claimed to be mentally unstable to stand trial and hence was placed in the Dodge Correctional Institute, then known as the Central State Hospital for the Criminally Insane. This was located in Waupan, Wisconsin, and was a place of high security. He was later transferred to Mendota State Hospital in Madison, where he was diagnosed as suffering from schizophrenia.

During 1968, upon examination, health authorities claimed that Gein was mentally stable enough to interact with his counselors and stand in court for his defense. The trial began in the beginning of November and continued for the next seven days. Gein's psychiatrist spoke in his defense by claiming that Gein was unaware of whether the murder of Bernice Worden was intentionally committed or was merely an accident. According to Gein's version of the incident, he was studying a gun in Worden's hardware store which accidentally fired, causing the murder. Gein claimed that he was trying to load a bullet in it and, while doing so, the rifle fired accidentally. According to him, the gun was not aimed at Worden, and any other detail was beyond his recall.

On November 14, Gein was found guilty of murder by the court. Another trial followed shortly, where doctors and mental authorities testified in Gein's defense against the prosecution and pled not guilty by reason of insanity. The court then passed the judgment that Gein was not guilty due to insanity and ordered for his transfer to the Central State Hospital for the Criminally Insane. Gein later spent the remaining years of his life in the mental hospital. It was stated by the judge, Robert H. Gollmar from the court of Waushara County that he was tried only for the murder of Bernice Worden due to prohibitive costs and had later confessed to having killed Mary Hogan as well.

After Gein's arrest, it was said that his

house and property were to be named as an attraction for tourists and was put up for auctioning in 1958. During the end of March 1958, the house was demolished due to fire, although no justified reasons have been cited for its destruction, apart from arson. When Gein was informed of this news during detention, he shrugged it off, hardly showing any remorse or emotion. Gein's car, which he had used to carry the corpses, was sold off in an auction for 760 dollars to a carnival manager, Bunny Gibbons. Gibbons later displayed the car in the carnival, for citizens to view upon a payment of 25 cents.

Death and Popular Usage

Gein died on July 26, 1984, of lung cancer induced liver and respiratory failure at Mendota Mental Health institute, being 77 years old. His grave was situated at the Plainfield Cemetery and was frequently damaged, with the gravestone being cut off piece by piece. During 2000, the entire gravestone was stolen and was recovered in 2001 in Seattle. It has since then been kept safely at the Sheriff's Department of Waushara County.

Even after his confinement, Ed Gein's story left an impact on many in America and found a place in several films and literature as well as music. One of the first works based on him was the novel 'Psycho', written by Robert Bloch and released in 1959, gaining huge popularity. It was a suspense thriller and fictional modification of the original events. The novel was made into a film of the same name by Alfred Hitchcock in 1960. The story of Ed Gein also found its way in small mentions in several other films like 'House of 1000 Corpses, the Sequel' and 'The Devil's Rejects', both by Rob Zombie; 'Ed Gein: The Butcher of Plainfield' (2007), 'Deranged' (1974), 'In The Light of The Moon' (2000) and 'Hitchcock' (2012). Gein was also used as the basic foundation for several other fiction-based serial killer characters, like Buffalo Bill ('The Silence of The Lambs'), Dr. Oliver Thredsen ('American Horror Story: Asylum'), Leatherface ('The Texas Chainsaw Massacre') and Norman Bates ('Psycho').

Filmmakers Errol Morris and Werner Herzog from Germany attempted to work on a collaboration, a documentary project about Gein, from 1975 to 1976. Gein was interviewed by Morris a number of times, and Morris took almost a year in questioning a number of locals and inhabitants of Plainfield. The two had even decided to exhume Gein's mother, Augusta, from her grave in order to test for a popular theory. However, the project never happened and the duo terminated their collaboration. In a profile about Errol Morris, published in 1989 in The New Yorker, this failed collaboration and its details were mentioned.

During the time Ed Gein's case was highly reported, there was an origination of the genre of black humor or black comedy. Gein's reference has been used several times in shock rock cultures and transgressive art types which only emphasized the sheer impact of his name or mention, but never looked into his life and crimes beyond that. Some of the notable mentions include a track by the band Slayer, 'Dead Skin Mask', from their 1990 album 'Seasons in the Abyss'. Another included the song 'Nothing to Gein' from the 2001 album of the band Mudvayne titled 'L.D. 50', and another track from the album 'Rusty Never Sleeps' by The Ziggens' in 1992, titled 'Ed Gein'. Another musical work which had a satirical feature of the murders and crimes committed by Ed Gein included on the album 'Soup' of 1995 by the group, Blind Melon, was their track 'Skinned'. The track played subtle mentions of Gein's murders, which were fictionalized to a certain extent, and ended with a touch of black humor with a background of cheerful instrumentals.

4. AILEEN WUORNOS

"I robbed them, and I killed them as cold as ice, and I would do it again, and I know I would kill another person because I've hated humans for a long time"
- Aileen Wuornos

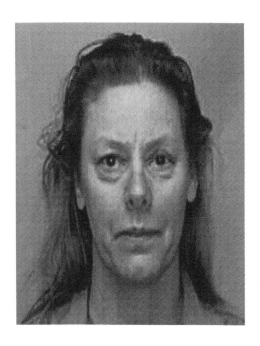

Aileen Carol Wuornos was a female serial murderer from the United States who murdered seven people, all men, from 1989 to 1990 in Florida. According to Wuornos, these killings were committed by her as a defense against rape or attempted rape during her days of working as a prostitute. The murders were committed by shooting at point blank range. Right before her execution, however, Wuornos confessed that she had murdered the men from whom she stole, and the killings were not merely an act of defending herself. Hence, the men whom she murdered had possessed some amount of money or wealth, as perceived by Wuornos. She was executed by lethal injection in 2002 after being sentenced to death for six murders.

Background and Early Life

Aileen Carol Pittman was born on February 29, 1956, in Rochester, Michigan, and later converted to her mother's maiden name Wuornos. Her mother, Diane Wuornos, was of mixed Finnish and American descent. Aileen's sibling, her brother Keith, was born in 1955.

Leo Dale Pittman was imprisoned due to sexual assault of children at the time of his daughter's birth and was also a schizophrenic. Hence, Wuornos never got the opportunity to meet or interact with her father. On January 30, 1969, her father committed suicide in prison, by hanging himself. When Aileen was around four years old, their mother left them in January. During March 1960, Aileen and her elder brother, Keith, were then legally adopted by their grandparents.

When she was 11 years old, Aileen became involved in sexual activities in school, for which she got food, drugs and cigarettes in return. She also engaged in sexual activities with her elder brother. According to Wuornos, her grandfather was addicted to drinking and would beat her violently as a child and would forcefully remove her clothes before committing these actions. When she was 14, Wuornos was raped by her grandfather's friend, and became pregnant in 1970. The illegitimate male child was born in March 23, 1971, in a home for unmarried mothers. The child was later taken for adoption. After her grandmother died due to liver failure, Wuornos left her school and was eventually thrown out of the house by her grandfather. When she was 15 years old, Wuornos began to earn a living by working as a prostitute and resided near her home in the forest.

Early Crimes

Wuornos was involved in crimes from the age of 18. She was arrested for driving recklessly, firing a gun from a car, and for misconduct in Colorado on May 27, 1974.

During 1976, Wuornos travelled to Florida where she met the president of a yacht club, 69 years of age, who would be her husband, Lewis Gratz Fell. They married and news of their marriage found a place in the society pages of the neighborhood papers. Unfortunately, Wuornos constantly was involved in confrontations and assaults and was later imprisoned for the same. Fell had to issue an order of restraint against Wuornos after she hit him with his own cane during an argument. She then went back to Michigan where she further became involved in minor crimes.

She was arrested in Antrim County after another scuffle at a local bar where she hit a bartender by throwing a ball while playing pool and hitting him on his head on July 14, 1976. Three days later, her elder brother passed away due to cancer in the esophagus, the result of which Wuornos received an insurance payment of ten thousand dollars. After nine weeks of togetherness, on July 21, Fell and Wuornos put an end to their marriage. Wuornos again got charged with drunk driving for which she had to a pay a fine of 105 dollars. Wuornos then proceeded to use the money from the insurance which she had received upon the death of Keith to pay the fine. She ended up squandering the rest of the money within a matter of two months, by spending on luxuries such as a new car, which she damaged within a short span of time.

Wuornos was arrested on May 20, 1981, for stealing cigarettes and money from a store in Edgewater, Florida. On May 4, 1982, she was imprisoned then later released in July of the following year. Another arrest followed when Wuornos passed forged cheques in a bank located at Key West, Florida, on May 1, 1984. She was also convicted for stealing a revolver and cartridges in another area on November 30, 1985.

Wuornos was arrested yet again, this time in Miami, on January 4, 1986. She was charged with resisting an arrest after having robbed a car. She gave an identification which bore the name of her aunt, hence, obstructing justice. The police authorities of Miami also recovered a pistol and some cartridges in the car which she had stolen. She was held for questioning in the state of Florida by the sheriff for assaulting a man in his car with a gun and demanding money on June 2, 1986. It was later found out upon examination that Wuornos was found to have carried extra ammunition and a pistol under the seat of the car of her victim.

She became friends with a hotel maid she met in a gay bar in Daytona, Tyria Moore. They eventually began living together, with Wuornos supporting them from whatever she earned from her job as a prostitute. They were later arrested for causing injuries with a beer bottle in the bar, and were held for questioning by the police at Daytona Beach. On March 12, 1988, Wuornos was pushed from a bus at Daytona Beach by the bus driver after a brief scuffle, and accused him of assaulting her. Moore claimed to have witnessed the situation. Wuornos continued to proclaim her love for Moore, even until the time of her execution.

Murders

During the time between the years 1989 and 1990, Wuornos murdered seven individuals, all of them male. Her first victim was Richard Mallory, 51 years old. He was the owner of an electronics store in Florida. Wuornos claimed to have killed him as an act of self-defense, on November 30, 1989. Mallory had been previously charged with rape. After two days, the sheriff of Volusia County, Florida, found Mallory's car. The corpse was recovered in December, some distance away in the woods, with multiple shots in his left lung. Wuornos was initially convicted of this murder.

The next victim was 43-year-old David Spears, who was employed in construction work in Winter Garden, Florida. His body was found in June 1, 1990 with six bullet wounds.

The body of Charles Carskaddon, 40 years old, was killed on March 31, 1990. His body was found in Florida, in Pasco County. Nine gunshot wounds were found in his body, believed to have been fired from a small-calibre gun.

Another victim was Peter Siems, a retired merchant marine, aged 65 years old, who was dedicated to the ministry of the church. On July 4, 1990, his abandoned car was recovered in Orange Springs, Florida. Though the body was never recovered, witnesses reported to have spotted the two, Wuornos and Moore, when they abandoned the car. Wuornos's palm print was discovered on a door handle of the car. Siems was said to have set off to drive from Jupiter, Florida, to New Jersey.

Troy Burress was a 50 year old who sold sausages in Ocala, Florida. He disappeared mysteriously on June 31, 1990. The next month, his corpse was recovered from the woods, with two gunshot wounds, in Marion County, Florida, on State Road 19.

The next victim was Charles 'Dick' Humphreys, 56 years old, who was killed on September 11th, 1990. He was a retired Major in the Air Force and had also worked previously as an investigator for State Child Abuse. His corpse was recovered the next day in Marion County, in full uniform, with six shots to the torso and head. His abandoned car was recovered in Suwannee County, Florida.

The final victim was Walter Jeno Antonio, 52 years of age, who was a truck driver, police reservist and a security guard. His body was found on a logging road in Dixie County, Florida on November 19, 1990. The body bore four gunshot wounds. His vehicle was recovered in Brevard County.

Capture and Trial

On July 4, 1990, Moore and Wuornos left the car they had stolen after murdering Siems when they caused an accident. Passersby who had witnessed the scene reported it to the police, describing the situation and their identities. This led to a campaign by the media to hunt the duo. The authorities recovered items owned by Siems in local hock shops and were able to match the fingerprints on the receipts with those found in his car. Wournos's fingerprints were already present with the police due to her criminal background in Florida.

The following year, on January 9, Wuornos was finally arrested in Volusia County. The following day, the police also arrested her partner, Tyria Moore, in Scranton, Pennsylvania. The police came to an agreement with her wherein she would compel Wuornos to confess. If she was successful, she would receive protection from being prosecuted in court. The police, along with Moore, came back to Florida. With help from the police, Moore continuously tried to contact Wuornos via telephone in order to clear her name. Wuornos finally confessed to all the murders on January 16, 1991, wherein she claimed that she had killed all the men as an act of self-defense because, according to her, the men had raped her.

Wuornos appeared in court for killing her first victim, Richard Mallory, on January 14, 1992. Previous crimes usually were not taken into consideration during criminal trials. However, as per the 'Williams rule' of Florida, it was permitted for the prosecution to bring forward the information of her previous criminal record in order to prove a criminal pattern. Based on confessions by Moore, Wuornos was found guilty for the murder of

Mallory on January 27. During her sentencing, psychologists speaking in the defense of Wuornos claimed that she was not mentally stable and was suffering from several psychological disorders. Wuornos received a death sentence after four days.

On March 31, 1992, Wuornos filed a no contest plea for committing three of her seven murders. She claimed that out of the three, Mallory had raped her violently while the others had attempted to rape her. Wuornos received death sentences for these three killings during the following May.

In June, Wuornos agreed to plead guilty for another murder, that of Charles Carkskaddon and, during November, received another death sentence. The defense claimed that Mallory was a convicted rapist and had been previously tried and convicted for the same. He was confined to a maximum security prison in Maryland that claimed to rehabilitate sexual offenders. From institutional records, it was proved that Mallory was undergoing therapy as he had been previously charged with sexual assault and rape and was confined to the facility for eight years. Hence, according to the defense, Mallory possessed sociopathic tendencies. However, the court still denied

Wuornos's retrial and refused to accept the evidence presented by the defense.

In 1993, Wuornos confessed and pled guilty for killing Antonio and received another death sentence. For the final murder, she received no charges, as the corpse was not recovered, giving Wuornos a total of six death sentences.

Afterwards, Wuornos gave several justifications for the murders which she had committed. At first, she had stated that all seven men whom she had murdered were rapists, and she had killed them as an act of self-defense. She later denied this and claimed that she killed them in the desire to steal from them and did not want to leave any witnesses behind. The filmmaker Nick Broomfield had interviewed her while she believed the cameras were off, and she stated that all of her murders were truly acts of self-defense, but she wanted to end her life after spending twelve years on death row.

Execution

Wuornos was imprisoned in Florida Department of Corrections Broward Correctional Institution, then she later was moved to Florida State Prison for her execution. Her appeal was denied in 1996 by the U.S.

Supreme Court. She had filed a petition in 2001 to the Florida Supreme Court, where she asked to fire her legal counsel, as well as end all the appeals which were pending. According to her, she had killed all those men in cold blood, on purpose, and had robbed them intentionally. She believed that she would commit those crimes again, hence it was useless to keep Wuornos alive. Even though she had been tested and studied thoroughly, she still felt that she had an intense hatred for humanity, which was inevitable as it 'crawls in her system'. Her attorneys felt that she unable, psychologically, to make such a petition; however, Wuornos felt that she had full knowledge of what she was asking, and even her psychologists agreed that her decision should be honored.

She believed, during 2002, that the prison workers had contaminated the meals with urine, dirt and saliva. She claimed that she had eavesdropped on a conversation between prison workers that they tried to push her to the brink of her tolerance and compel her to kill herself before her execution and that some of them wanted to rape her. She also felt that other acts were committed purposefully as an act of hatred towards her, like kicking her prison door, handcuffing her hands too tightly, decreased pressure of water, mold in her sleeping mattress, sudden and excessive window checks, and taunting her with lewd gestures. She claimed that she would boycott offers of food and showers when the certain workers were on duty, and her attorney supported her by claiming that Wuornos desired proper, humane treatment before she was executed and that she was fully aware of what she was saying.

Wuornos was executed on October 9, 2002. She was pronounced dead at 9:47 AM. She wanted chicken as her final meal, which was within twenty-dollar limit, but was content with having just coffee. Her final words were, "Yes, I would just like to say I'm sailing with the rock, and I'll be back, like Independence Day with Jesus, June 6, like the movie. Big mother ship and all, I'll be back, I'll be back."

Before she was executed, Wuornos had several interviews with filmmaker Broomfield. In her last interview, she claimed again that she faced harassment at her correctional institute. She felt that in order to make her feel even more helpless, the food and torture became worse every time she attempted to lodge a complaint. She blamed societal stereotypes and the media for the execution of a rape victim without showing any consideration for her condition.

After the cremation of Wuornos's body, her ashes were returned to her hometown in Michigan by Dawn Botkins and scattered beneath a tree. Wuornos's final request was that the song 'Carnival' by Natalie Merchant be played during her funeral. The film maker, Broomfield, later tried to speculate how Wuornos must have felt mentally and the reasons behind her actions. He believed that working as a prostitute made her face many unpleasant experiences, and a certain amount of anger and wrath had built up within her due to those experiences. With time, he believed that this anger increased and was expressed in the form of violence in due time. He felt that this anger prevented her from distinguishing between something which could endanger a life and a minor argument, which is what led to her extreme expression of anger. When she wasn't in such extreme behaviors, he believed that Wuornos was at heart a compassionate person.

In Popular Culture

The case of Wuornos was mentioned briefly by FBI agent, Robert K. Ressler, in his autobiography, citing his experience in the FBI during the last twenty years. During 1992, he had mentioned that he never talked much about women who were serial killers as he believed they killed all at once instead of maintaining any consistency. He felt, however, that Wuornos was an exception. Wuornos's story found a place in other books as well, such as 'Lethal Intent', by Sue Russell. 'Dear Dawn: Aileen Wuornos in her Own Words' was the title of a compilation of letters written by her to her closest acquaintance, Dawn Botkins. They were edited and compiled by Lisa Kester and Daphne Gottlieb in 2012. The filmmaker Nick Broomfield made two biographies regarding Wuornos, which included 'Aileen Wuornos: The Selling of a Selling Serial', and 'Aileen: Life and Death of a Serial Killer', released in the years 1993 and 2003. Wuornos's story was also telecasted in several television series, such as 'Deadly Women' and 'American Justice, Biography'.

The story of Aileen Wuornos was showcased into a film in 1992, 'Overkill: The Aileen Wuornos Story' starring Jean Smart in the role of Aileen. The second film about her had Charlize Theron playing the role of Wuornos in the film 'Monster', released in 2003. Theron won an Academy Award for this film, for her role as Wuornos.

Aileen Wuornos was mentioned in several musical numbers as well, such as

'Nicotine Love' by Jewel, and also 'Sixth of June' by the metal core musical group, 'It Dies Today', based in New York. A poem titled as her full name was written by the poet Doron Braunshtein, an audio version of which is present in a CD titled 'The Obsessive Poet'. Another poem also finds its place in the 2005 publication of Arsenal Pulp Press, titled Red Light, Superheroes, Saints and Sluts, which is Rima Banerji's poem titled 'Sugar Zero' and was dedicated to Aileen Wuornos, and. Wuornos's fictionalized story was also mentioned within 'American Horror Story: Hotel' during episode four shown on television.

5. JANE TOPPAN

The Nightmare Nurse

"That is my ambition, to have killed more people, more helpless people, than any man or woman who has ever lived."

Jane Toppan, also known as Jolly Jane, was a female serial killer with one of the strangest case histories. It is known that she herself had confessed to the 33 murders she had committed in 1901 and, in her statement, she had said that her goal was to kill more helpless people than anyone who ever lived. As a nurse, she gave lethal morphine injections to patients to kill them. She would have gone on committing even more murders if she was not caught after poisoning the Davis family. She was finally arrested in 1901, but her repeated attempts at killing herself landed her in a mental hospital. She lived in the mental hospital for 40 years before she finally breathed her last. Jane Toppan definitely remains one of the most horrifying serial killers to date.

Background and Early Life

Jane Toppan was born in 1857 to Irish parents as Honora Kelley. Her mother, Bridget Kelley, died when she was a little girl. It is known that she was suffering from tuberculosis before her death. She left the little girl with an alcoholic father, Peter Kelley, who was known to his acquaintances as "Kelley the Crack" because of his eccentric nature. Honora had a troubled childhood living with an insane, alcoholic father and, though she lived with him only for a few years, these formative years had a psychological impact upon her. She lived with Kelley for a few years in dire poverty before Kelley brought her and her sister, Delia, to Boston Female Asylum, an orphanage, in 1863. He refused to take any responsibility for the children. After living there for a few years,

Honora was taken as an indentured servant by a woman named Mrs. Ann Toppan living in Lowell, Massachusetts. She was never officially adopted by this family, but Honora was given the surname. It is here that Honora got her new identity as Jane Toppan. It may have been a conscious decision to change the name because there was an ongoing prejudice against Irish immigrants during that time. Therefore, hiding her roots seemed the best option at hand for a young girl like her. She grew up to be extremely jealous of her pretty young stepsister.

She started getting aggressive from late adolescence and made two suicide attempts. Her troubled childhood and abnormal behavior as an adolescent led to her insanity and psychological problems later in life. She became convinced that nobody would ever want to marry her and left home in 1885 to become a nurse. She enrolled as a nursing student at a hospital in Cambridge, Massachusetts, from where she began her career as a serial killer.

Murders

Jane was trained in nursing and she was undoubtedly an excellent nurse. Though she avoided getting caught due to lack of security and proper examination during those times, but there were doubts among the authorities regarding her odd ways of treatment and her excessive fascination with autopsies. During her tenure as a nurse at the Cambridge Hospital, Jane began treating her patients as guinea pigs by experimenting on them with several drugs.

The place where she was working had low security, and she was mostly left to do whatever she pleased without much risk of getting caught. She started using drugs like Atropine and Morphine on patients whom she disliked. She felt a certain delight in killing her patients with these drugs, and she never got caught. She was known to everyone as "Jolly Jane" because of her cheerful nature and her interest in giving so much of her time to her patients. Apparently, it seemed that she was a dedicated nurse giving all her time and attention to the betterment of her patients. Her employers and co-workers were, however, unaware of the fact that the time she dedicated to her patients was utilized in something other than taking care of them. Jane made fake charts to deceive people while using several drugs to bring her patients in and out of consciousness and often injecting lethal drugs to kill them. Nobody knew the evil designs or the horrifying psychology behind the calm, cheerful and benevolent face of a nurse. No wonder she began to be referred to later in newspaper reports as the 'Angel of Death'. She confessed after her arrest that she derived a certain sexual thrill when she saw her patients being so near death. She would choose her victims, give them a lethal mixture of drugs and lie in bed with them, holding them close to her as they neared death.

This kind of a sexual attraction is quite uncommon for female serial killers who usually commit murders for robbery and other kinds of material gain. It is indeed repulsive how a nurse began to cherish the act of bringing her patients in and out of coma and unconsciousness and making them swing like a pendulum between life and death for her pleasure. It is difficult to fathom the reason which made her act in such a manner. In her confession, Jane had revealed once that she had, in fact, studied nursing only to learn how to kill people and to get the chance to do so. However shocking it may sound, it was indeed a case of extremely twisted and perverted psychology which made her act in such a manner.

In 1889, she joined the Massachusetts General Hospital where she once again selected several victims whom she recklessly killed in the same manner. Her services were in great demand because of her outward nature, but her patients would seldom survive her care and treatment. In 1890, she was fired by the Massachusetts General Hospital because of the deaths of an unusually high number of patients. She was actually fired on the charges of negligence when the patients died of morphine overdoses, but her real intentions were still masked back then. These would become the subject of speculation much later in her career. She returned to Cambridge Hospital for a very brief period before being dismissed from there too on account of recklessly prescribing opiates to her patients.

Thereafter, she began working as a private duty nurse to sustain herself as well as continue her thrill for murder. She was accused several times of charges of petty theft, but it wasn't enough to stop her from getting further employment. She continued to work as a private nurse every now and then and went on killing people in secretive ways. In fact, she was quite popular in New England during those days as a dedicated and caring nurse, and people were constantly seeking her out to take care of their ailing family members. While there were frequent deaths, nobody kept a count or suspected anything.

In 1895, she took her murdering spree to a new level when she killed her landlords by poisoning. In 1899, Elizabeth, her foster sister, was killed with strychnine poisoning just because she disliked the girl. In 1901, she started living with the Davis family to take care of an elderly man called Alden Davis. She was hired to take care of the elderly man after the death of his wife, who was incidentally murdered by Jane herself. Within a few weeks of living with this family at Cataumet, she had killed Mr. Davis as well as his two daughters, Annie Gordon and Mary Gibbs. Mr. Davis was said to have died from a stroke, though his younger daughter Mary's death aroused suspicion.

Following this incident, she went back to her hometown and there she started to court the husband of her dead foster sister. When she failed to win his love, she decided to poison him and his sister so that she could prove her merit and concern as a nurse by taking care of him. Though his sister died of poisoning, he survived. To avoid being suspected, she even poisoned herself to rouse his sympathy for her, but her plan failed and he eventually threw her out of the house upon learning the reality.

Capture

The other living members of the Davis family were surprised to see healthy members of the family dying one by one. Mary Gibbs's husband suspected something was amiss and ordered a toxicology examination of the dead body of the youngest daughter of Alden Davis. A Harvard Medical School graduate was called upon for examination and investigation, and it was revealed in the report that the girl had been poisoned with lethal doses of Morphine. Soon the local authorities were informed, and they issued an arrest warrant against Jane Toppan. She was finally accused and arrested for murder charges on October 29, 1901, in Amherst, New Hampshire. If it was not for the Davis family members dying one by one unnaturally, Jane would have continued her murdering spree. Her killings at the Davis household cut short her career as one of America's most twisted and strangest of serial killers.

Trial and Sentencing

During her trial, she first denied killing anybody and said aloud that she wouldn't even kill a chicken ever. But the police suspected her due to the poison found in the body of Mary Gibbs. They investigated her previous records and traced a pharmacist from whom she got her regular supply of Morphine. Though there were several prescriptions for Morphine, further investigation revealed that they were false and all the signatures of the doctors were forged. On further interrogation, she confessed to having committed 31 murders, naming all of her victims. However, many still believe that the list of her victims number more than 70. There was never any accurate list of her victims in any records. She revealed that she felt a strange pleasure watching her victims die slowly in front of her. It was an insane pleasure that she derived from it and the only pleasure she loved to have.

She loved being at the side of her patients while they suffered painfully as their breathing stopped slowly and they died a slow death. She also revealed how she would erase the signs of Morphine poisoning, often by injecting Atropine to dilate the pupils of those victims. This would make doctors less suspicious about the cause of death and it gave her chances to escape from being exposed.

Her lawyer finally conceded 11 murders and pleaded insanity of his client. Jane's own statement moved the court to declare her insane. She was sentenced for life and sent to the Taunton Insane Hospital where she lived until the last day of her life. Some say that her insanity was hereditary as her father and her sister both suffered from insanity during their lifetime.

During her days in the asylum, she developed a mania from her unnatural desire to poison people. She started to believe that all her doctors, lawyers and attendants were planning to kill her. She began to decline food in fear of being poisoned and lost a lot of weight, which severely deteriorated her health. She began to be haunted by her ill past. Finally, in August 1938, at the age of 84, she breathed her last. Some of her keepers remembered her as a quiet old lady. Some of her older attendants, however, recalled her smile as she beckoned them into her room and asked them to bring some morphine so they could have fun watching people die.

Case Study

Jane Toppan definitely features in the list of the most terrifying serial killers of all times. She is, at the same time, also the strangest and the most bizarre case of the lot. Every serial killer usually has a motive of revenge, lust, greed or sexual perversion; Jane had none. It is true, as per her confession, that she liked to hold her victims close to her in bed as they neared death. Her victims were neither her real enemies, nor in fancy or in a state of schizophrenia. She had no grudge against her victims. They had usually liked her and been kind to her, and she would gain nothing by killing them.

According to Toppan herself, she did not remember the details of murder in each case, but she confessed that poisoning had become a habit of her daily life. She loved to poison and kill without any malice or valid motive. The method of killing was mostly the same in each case. She always used a lethal dose of Morphine and, in some cases, she brought about death by administering a dose of Atropine. As a nurse, she played and experimented with drugs on her patients, but Morphine remained her choice of drug almost every time because it gave her the route to escape. Morphine paralyzed the breathing of the patients, killing them slowly, which gave the impression that the patient must have died from natural causes. Due to the lack of thorough examination during those times, this trick gave her the route to escape unscathed each and every time.

In spite of being a cheerful person and a trained nurse, Toppan's life was tainted by one dangerous secret passion, and that was to bring slow death to her victims. She developed a kind of affection for her patients and yet had a paradoxical desire to take them towards death instead of recovery. Her feelings, however, never crossed the flirtation stage, as before they could grow, she would have become tired and finished off her chosen victim. This is an extremely strange case that has puzzled many. Only a very few in her medical career seemed to have survived the care of this smiling nurse with ghastly intentions. One of her surviving victims was O.M. Brigham, the husband of her foster sister whom she had killed by poisoning. Soon after his wife's death, he too was stricken by a strange malady. During the period Jane nursed him, his condition varied from day to day. Sometimes he would be nearly dead while on other days he would start recovering. He kept going in and out of unconsciousness until Jane decided to let him live.

Her moral insanity worsened later in life and even had adverse psychological effects. Due to her misdeeds and crimes committed, she began to have serious trust issues during her last days. She became schizophrenic and suffered from unshakeable beliefs that she would eventually be poisoned and killed by her doctors and attendants for revenge. During her initial days in the asylum, she seemed perfectly sane, and people even questioned the reason why she was kept there in the Taunton asylum as she looked as sane as her attendants. However, traces of insanity became visible later as her delusions became more frequent, then constant.

She lost her previous cheerful demeanor and transformed into an old, ugly and delirious woman who would be suspicious of everything and everyone. Her refusal to consume food, believing she would be poisoned, led to her eventual death as her health started failing and she dwindled to a skeleton. It can be said that her intellectual insanity resulted from her moral insanity and this accelerated her death. It was reported that her lack of understanding of morality and natural feelings, and her lack of control from committing crimes are proofs of her moral insanity. She neither expressed bravado for her acts of crime nor did she show any remorse or repentance. During her trial, she herself couldn't understand the reason why she failed to repent for her deeds. It can be said that she had developed a strange psychology over the years which eliminated her sense of right and wrong and did not let her feel natural emotions of guilt, remorse or repentance. The sexual angle involved in this case also heightened the reason to suspect moral insanity of the woman. Her unusual case of sexual pleasure being derived from seeing people die was the biggest proof of her lack of moral understanding and a perverse psychology aloof from normality and the society around her.

Cases of sexual sadism have usually been seen in males, but this strange behavior in a female serial killer was indeed rare and shocking. This is why this case shook one and all and interested not only legal and medical practitioners but the common public as well. People were astonished reading about her arrest and confession in print.

Fictional Portrayals

This mysterious lady serial killer is believed to have inspired the character "the incomparable Bessie Denker" in the book *The Bad Seed* by William March. Denker, like Toppan, began poisoning people from a young age. Maxwell Anderson later turned this novel into a play and a film that were quite successful.

The 2002, Jon Keeyes and Debbie Rochon came out with an independent film called *American Nightmare* where a mentally unstable serial killer called Jane Toppan stalks and kills seven young people. This ghastly murderess also plays the role of a nurse in the film and is said to be inspired by the real life character of Jane Toppan. An episode was devoted to Jane Toppan in each of the shows, *Deadly Women* and *Criminal*.

In the play called *Murderess*, written by Anne Bertram, Jane Toppan featured in one of the monologues. The play premiered at St. Paul, Minnesota, and this particular segment was called 'The Truth About Miss Toppan' where Laura Wiebers played the role of the nurse. The well-known critic named William Randall Beard referred to this segment as a "chilling portrait of a sociopath nurse".

Several books and characters, whether fictional or non-fictional, have traces of Jane Toppan. A book called 'The Case of Jane Toppan and Erzsebet Bathory (Sexual Sadism)' by Steven G. Carley discusses the lives and psychology of these women along with a few other strange cases.

6. NANNIE DOSS
The Giggling Granny

If there is a need to list the most shocking and the deadliest women serial killers of all times, the list should definitely feature the name of Nannie Doss. This woman with an apparently cheerful frame of mind committed the most gruesome murders of 11 people, mostly her family members, and has one of the most repulsive and spine-chilling case histories ever. Due to her murder records, she has earned herself a number of popular names like 'Giggling Nannie', 'Giggling Grandma', 'The Black Widow', 'Lonely Hearts Killer', 'Arsenic Annie', etc. In 1954, she confessed her crimes when her fifth husband died and she was finally arrested. She received a life sentence in 1964 but died the following year due to leukemia.

Background and Early Life

Nannie Doss was born as Nancy Hazel in Blue Mountain, Alabama, on November 4, 1905. She was born to Louisa and James F. Hazel and had four siblings, three sisters and one brother. It can be said that Nancy suffered a troubled childhood because her father was an abusive and controlling man. She and her mother both hated him immensely for his behavior. The little girl's childhood naturally turned traumatic due to the presence of such a father. Moreover, the financial condition of the family was poor. The father forced the children to work on the farm instead of attending school or studying. Nancy was a poor student anyway and never excelled in her studies, and this erratic kind of education due to her disturbed family hampered it further.

At the age of 7, she was on a trip to

South Alabama to visit her relatives. The train in which she was travelling met with an accident and stopped suddenly. Nancy hit her head on a metal bar in this accident which caused her to suffer for a few years. She started having blackouts and headaches for a long time which pushed her into depression. She later said that this incident during her formative years had a role to play in her later mental instability.

Her childhood hobby was reading romantic magazines from her mother's collection, and she started fantasizing about a romantic future ahead. All the four sisters of the family led disturbed teenage lives under their controlling father. Though she dreamt of a romantic future, she, along with her sisters, was forbidden by their father from wearing attractive dresses and makeup on their faces. He gave the reason that he was protecting them from getting molested by men at a young age, but it was just a part of his controlling, patriarchal nature. He could not prevent Nancy from getting molested on a couple of occasions by some local men during her teenage years. He curbed their social lives, too, by stopping them from attending dances, parties and other social events. The girls led secluded lives without mixing freely.

In 1921, at the early age of 16, she married a man called Charley Braggs at the insistence of her father. She had known him for about four months before her marriage. She and Charley worked at the Linen Thread factory and knew each other there. With her father approving the proposal, they got married soon although she hardly knew much about him. Her first husband, Charley Braggs, lived with his mother and was her only son. His mother had never married and continued to live with her son even after his marriage. Doss hated her mother-in-law, and it is clear from her confession later in life where she recounts how the woman took complete control over her life after the marriage. She found no fault with her son and took a lot of his attention. She had even curbed Doss's activities in order to control her, which seriously irked the young bride. From this marriage, she had four daughters between 1923 and 1927.

An unhappy marriage and the burden of four children at such a young age took a toll on her mental and physical condition and stressed her out. Physically and emotionally drained, she took to smoking and drinking and soon was addicted. She and her spouse both suspected and accused each other of infidelity. Her husband disappeared for days at a stretch without any notice. In 1927, the two middle girls died of food poisoning. It is suspected that Doss had killed her own daughters back then. Braggs was frightened and suspected how the two healthy children died within a few months of each other. He recalled seeing them healthy when he left for work, but they soon died from convulsions after breakfast. Braggs fled away with the first daughter, Melvina, and the youngest girl, Florine, was left with Nannie. She began working in a cotton mill to support herself and her daughter. Her mother-in-law had passed away by then. A year later, Braggs came back with Melvina and divorced Nannie. She then took away both her girls and went back to her mother, leaving her husband. Braggs, however, always said that he left Nannie because he was scared of the woman.

After returning to her mother in Anniston, Alabama, Doss started living there with her two daughters. She started gaining interest once again in romances and took to reading True Romance and such other magazines. The Lonely Hearts column particularly interested her, and she began writing to men who advertised there. In this manner, she met Robert Franklin Harrelson, or

Frank, living in Jacksonville. He was a 23-year-old young man who was employed in a factory. They started dating each other by exchanging cakes and poems. In 1929, at the age of 24, two years after the divorce from Braggs, Nannie married Frank and moved to Jacksonville to live with him along with her two daughters, Melvina and Florine. They stayed together for 16 years even though Frank was an alcoholic man with a record of assault.

Murders

One of the first murders she was suspected to have committed was of her grandchild. Melvina gave birth to her first son in 1943 and a second child in 1945 that died very soon. The young girl, in a distressed state due to labor and ether, believed that she saw her mother poking a hatpin into the baby's head. She could not make out whether she was seeing a real picture or imagining, and she asked others for clarification. Her husband and her sister told her how Doss had reported that the baby was dead, but they too recalled seeing her with a pin. The doctors failed to give any explanation for the death, and this led to Doss escaping unpunished. Melvina and her husband were distraught after the death of the newborn baby and soon drifted apart. Heartbroken, Melvina got involved with a soldier whom Nannie disliked very much. Mother and daughter were cross with each other because of this incident and fought bitterly.

In 1945, when Florine went to visit her father, leaving her son Lee with her mother, the young boy died. It is suspected that the child died due to asphyxia and his grandmother was behind it. The baby's death aroused suspicions, but it was claimed that the baby had accidentally got hold of some rat poison and consumed it. After two months, Nannie collected $500 from the life insurance she carried on the baby.

In 1945, after killing her grandchildren, it was time for her to kill her husband Frank too. In 1945, when Japan lost the war, Frank was one of those people who partied frequently. One evening, he drank heavily, came home and raped Nannie. The rape was the final event she would tolerate in the marriage, and the next day she poisoned his corn whiskey jar with rat poison. Frank painfully died that evening after drinking from the jar.

After the death of her second husband Frank, Nannie took once again to the Lonely Hearts column. Through this column she met her third husband, Arlie Lanning, while she was travelling in North Carolina. She married this man three days later, but he too turned out to be as alcoholic as her last husband. In fact, Arlie was a womanizer, and he must have convinced Nannie to marry him in that way. But in this marriage, it was Nannie and not Arlie who would disappear for days and months at a stretch. During the time she was at home, she played a perfect housewife to her husband. The man is said to have died from heart failure, and the entire town supported the widowed wife. Soon after the funeral of her husband, the house, which was left to Lanning's sister, was mysteriously burnt down. Nannie got the insurance money and kept it in her account. Soon after, Lanning's mother died in her sleep while Nannie was nursing the woman's broken hip. Two of her sisters, too, died one after the other in the following year while Nannie was visiting them. Both showed mysterious symptoms of convulsions and stomach-ache and died quickly.

It was time to search for another husband, and this time Nannie became a part of the Diamond Circle Club where she met her fourth husband, Richard L. Morton. This man, who lived in Emporia, Kansas, was not an alcoholic like her previous husbands, but he definitely was a womanizer. Morton died in April 1953, some months after Lou, Nannie's mother, had come down to stay with them, and she too died of being poisoned to death.

Nannie's last marriage was with a man called Samuel Doss of Tulsa, Oklahoma, two months after the death of her last husband. Samuel Doss was a clean, churchgoing man who disliked all the romances Nannie was fond of and fantasized about.

In September that year, Samuel was admitted to a hospital for flu, but he was also diagnosed with digestive tract infection. He was treated in that hospital and nursed back to good health before being released. On October 5, he was released from the hospital and came back home, but that very evening, he met his death when Nannie killed him in a hurry to collect two life insurance policies in his name. Only on that day did the effective dates on the policies overlap. The autopsy report of Samuel Doss alerted the authorities, and Nannie Doss was soon arrested on murder charges.

Capture
Doss had evaded punishment easily in all the previous murders she had committed due to negligence on the part of the other family members and the doctors. Nobody ever raised a

query even though things seemed suspicious. But this time, things were different when healthy and just released Samuel Doss died as soon as he reached home. The doctor who treated him smelled something fishy about the whole incident and immediately ordered an autopsy. The report stunned everyone as it showed cleared signs of arsenic poisoning, following which Doss was arrested. In fact, there was enough arsenic found in the man's body to kill about twenty people.

When Samuel Doss was admitted for the first time in the hospital, she had tried to poison him by mixing arsenic in his prune cake. She failed at the attempt, and the doctors nursed him back to health, though without suspecting any foul play. But the second time, she was successful in killing him by dosing his coffee severely with arsenic. This last murder became her undoing, and she confessed her crimes on being arrested by the police. Several bodies of her dead family members were then exhumed and examined, and each of them were reported to have either died from arsenic poisoning or rat poisoning.

Trial and Sentencing
After her arrest, Nannie Doss succumbed to the interrogation and confessed that she had

killed Samuel Doss in return for his refusal to let her keep her romance magazines. Soon she confessed one by one about all the murders she had committed secretly throughout her life. She recalled killing her four husbands, her mother and her sister, her mother-in-law and also her grandchildren. Since she was arrested in Oklahoma, the state centered the case only on the murder of Samuel Doss who had married Nannie through the Lonely Hearts Club advertisement after losing his family in a tornado. According to the prosecution, Nannie was perfectly fit and healthy for the trial. It was found during the proceedings that Samuel loved a certain sweet potato pie recipe made by Nannie, and she had taken the opportunity to lace it with arsenic thrice before his death on various occasions. She pled guilty before the court, but the court sentenced her to life imprisonment. She was saved from capital punishment only because she was a woman. She was also saved from the punishment of other murders due to lack of cases registered for them. In 1965, she died from leukemia in the Oklahoma State Penitentiary.

Case Study

Nannie Doss definitely features in the list of the highest rated female psycho serial killers of all times. When people learned about her, they were shocked because they could not fathom how a gruesome killer could be living behind the cheerful demeanor of a gentlewoman. On the outside, Nannie was a sweet-natured wife, an amiable neighbor and a good parent. But on the inside, there lived a psychopath, a cold-blooded murderer who eliminated her own family singlehandedly. She not only killed her husbands, but also her own mother and grandchildren. Money could have been the motive in several cases since she had banked all the insurance money she got after the deaths, but it was not the single motive in all the cases. This is clear from her confession where she said that her murders were triggered by disputes and marital boredom.

It can be said that she killed whenever there was an argument or whenever her husband became too controlling for her. She confessed that all her life she tried to find the ideal husband, the kind of husband she read about in the True Romance magazines, but never found such a person in the ones she had married. She said that she was searching all her life for the perfect mate who would bring her some romance in real life.

Analyzing her psychology, it can be said

that her early childhood accident may have had a role to play in her abnormality. According to the Psychopathology Model, which states that early childhood experiences may influence crimes later in life, the train accident in her early childhood could have been a cause behind this mental state. Being hit on the head, she suffered depression, headaches and blackouts, and such a traumatic period of stress in her early childhood could have developed severe anxiety disorders later in life, which contributed in her mental state to make her a psycho serial killer. Even though she herself blamed that incident in her life, she had no remorse when she was convicted nor did she plead insanity. She was, therefore, judged as perfectly sane and fit for trial. Her confession about the motive behind the murders shocked one and all, and she was even seen smiling after receiving the life sentence.

It is indeed shocking how an apparently softhearted woman seeking love and romance in her life could have so many skeletons hidden in her closet. It is difficult to imagine how such a woman could have continued murdering one family member after the other just in search of true romance in her life. Studying her life and psychology, it can be concluded that her childhood and teenage years were responsible for this bizarre and twisted psychology. She and her mother hated her father right from her childhood, as she had grown up seeing him as an abusive and controlling man. She, like her mother, buried herself in romances and Lonely Hearts columns just to forget the reality and live in a dream world. It is often seen that women who have suffered badly since childhood in a troubled family or under abusive fathers oftentimes end up hating the male gender so much in reality that they either become aggressive in their attitudes or try to repress the harsh reality by seeking escape in romances and fairy tales where everything seems good.

Nannie must have faced the same thing, and she grew up with the dream that she would soon get to meet her dream husband, one that she had read of in the romances. But her Prince Charming never arrived, and her husbands severely disappointed her. All she would get in reality were alcoholic, abusive men and womanizers. She suffered troubled married lives by being neglected, cheated, abused and even raped by her second husband. This may have had a severe impact on her already disturbed psyche and led her to eliminate each one of them and bury herself again in the

Lonely Hearts column in search of true romance. In one of her confessions, she recalls how she hated being controlled by her last husband, Samuel Doss, who restricted her from access to magazines, radio and television to make her lead the life of a true Christian woman. She got irked so much that she decided to lace his food with arsenic to kill him off. Her return to the Lonely Hearts column is a proof of her confession that she was looking for the right mate all her life. It shows how lonely and hopeful she had always been. Somehow all these impacts shaped her psychology in such a bizarre and horrific way over the years, producing one of the most shocking cold-blooded serial killers of all times.

How Nannie survived and escaped from being caught during the 28 years of poisoning several people in her family is surely unthinkable and a mystery to be solved. She was a self-made widow, earning the names 'Black Widow', 'Lonely Hearts Killer' and 'Giggling Nannie'. When questioned by the detectives, she maintained her cheerful demeanour, joked about her dead husbands, and told them that her conscience was quite clear. She had married them out of love and she had always dreamt her ideal mate to be a person of 'amour', just like she had seen in television and romance magazines. The jolly widow even told the detectives how she was still sure she would find the right mate someday.

Thank you to my editor, proofreaders, and cover artist for your support:

~ RJ

Aeternum Designs (book cover), Bettye McKee (editor), Lee Knieper Husemann, Lorrie Suzanne Phillippe, Marlene Fabregas, Darlene Horn, Ron Steed, Katherine McCarthy, Robyn MacEachern, Kathi Garcia, Linda H. Bergeron, Lynda Lata, Kali Bosworth, Tina Bates, Lorelei Pierce, Jennifer Janzen, Nancy Masterson

Serial Homicide (Volume 1)

Notorious Serial Killers Series

This is the first book in the 'Serial Homicide' series which will feature six notorious cases in each volume.

Ted Bundy was a burglar, rapist, kidnapper, necrophiliac (sexual intercourse with a corpse) and serial killer in the 1970s. It's believed he killed 30 plus women.

Jeffrey Dahmer (the Milwaukee Monster), was a rapist, killer, necrophiliac, and cannibal who killed 17 young boys and men between 1978 and 1991.

Albert Fish was a child rapist, cannibal and serial killer who operated between 1924 and 1932. It's believed that he killed at least 9 children and possibly more.

During the 1980s and '90s, **Gary Ridgway** (Green River Killer), a serial killer and necrophiliac, is believed to have killed 49 women, but confessed to murdering 71.

Between 1978 and 1983 in the United

Kingdom, **Dennis Nilsen** (The Kindly Killer) is known to have killed between 12 and 15 young men. He had a ritual of bathing and dressing the corpses, preserving them for a time before dissecting and disposing of his victims by either burning them in a fire or flushing their parts down a toilet.

Known as the Co-Ed Butcher, **Edmund Kemper** was a cannibal, necrophiliac and serial killer who, between 1964 and 1973, killed 10 women including his mother who he beheaded, used her head as a dartboard and for oral sex.

Plus... Bonus Story

In February 2013, LAPD Cop **Chris Dorner** went on a shooting revenge/spree killing targeting higher-up officers and their families.

Click for *eBook* **or** *Paperback*

About the Author

RJ Parker, Ph.D. is an award-winning and bestselling true crime author and owner of RJ Parker Publishing, Inc. He has written over 20 true crime books which are available in eBook, paperback and audiobook editions, and have sold in over 100 countries. He holds certifications in Serial Crime, Criminal

Profiling and a PhD in Criminology.

To date, RJ has donated over 3,000 autographed books to allied troops serving overseas and to our wounded warriors recovering in Naval and Army hospitals all over the world. He also donates to Victims of Violent Crimes Canada.

If you are a police officer, firefighter, paramedic or serve in the military, active or retired, RJ gives his eBooks freely in appreciation for your service.

Contact Information

Author's Email:

AuthorRJParker@gmail.com

Publisher's Email:

Agent@RJParkerPublishing.com

Website:

http://m.RJPARKERPUBLISHING.com/

Twitter:

http://www.Twitter.com/realRJParker

Facebook:

https://www.Facebook.com/AuthorRJParker

Amazon Author's Page:

rjpp.ca/RJ-PARKER-BOOKS

** SIGN UP FOR OUR MONTHLY
NEWSLETTER **

http://rjpp.ca/RJ-PARKER-NEWSLETTER

References

JOHN WAYNE GACY
http://www.biography.com/people/john-wayne-gacy-10367544
http://murderpedia.org/male.G/g1/gacy-john-wayne.htm

DENNIS RADER
http://dennisraderbtk.blogspot.ca/
http://www.crimeandinvestigation.co.uk/crime-files/dennis-rader-the-btk-killer

EDWARD THEODORE GEIN
http://www.houseofhorrors.com/gein.htm
http://murderpedia.org/male.G/g/gein-edward.htm
http://criminalminds.wikia.com/wiki/Ed_Gein

AILEEN WUORNOS
http://www.capitalpunishmentincontext.org/cases/wuornos
http://www.crimeandinvestigation.co.uk/crime-files/aileen-wuornos

JANE TOPPAN
http://womenserialkillers.blogspot.ca/2011/02/jane-toppan-nightmare-nurse.html

http://murderpedia.org/female.T/t/toppan-jane.htm

NANNIE DOSS

http://www.encyclopediaofalabama.org/article/h
-3619

http://gizmodo.com/the-giggling-granny-serial-
killer-who-smiled-all-the-1718086506

http://murderpedia.org/female.D/d/doss-
nannie.htm

25541444R00061

Made in the USA
Lexington, KY
23 December 2018